Barbara Baker

MW01056910

Technic Is Fun

EARLY ELEMENTARY   ELEMENTARY A

Selected Studies and Etudes
Compiled and Edited by

GAIL LEW

Graded Etude Collections from Standard Repertory

Technic Is Fun offers piano students a series of graded studies and etudes for the development of technic, style, and musicianship. These studies will reinforce the technical requirements found in method books and in standard piano repertory. The etudes found in this series not only build technic and musicality but also have been carefully selected to provide refreshing recital repertoire and to develop a strong musical and technical foundation.

Project Manager: Gail Lew
Cover Design: Martha Lucia Ramirez

© 2000 BELWIN-MILLS PUBLISHING CORP. (ASCAP)
This Edition © 2004 BELWIN-MILLS PUBLISHING CORP. (ASCAP)
All Rights Administered by WARNER BROS. PUBLICATIONS U.S. INC.
All Rights Reserved including Public Performance

Contents

Trumpet Tune

Staccato melody, legato accompaniment

DANIEL TÜRK
No. 1 from "Anfängerstücke für Klavier"

Bouncing Ball

Staccato study

DANIEL TÜRK
No. 2 from "Anfängerstücke für Klavier"

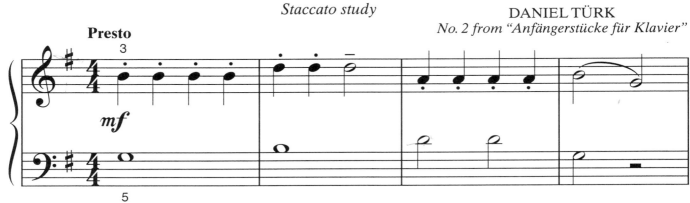

ELM00035A

Walking Along

Melody and accompaniment, balance between the hands

CORNELIUS GURLITT
Op. 187, No. 19

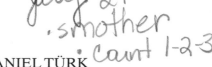

Marching in a Parade

Legato, staccato

DANIEL TÜRK
No. 3 from "Anfängerstücke für Klavier"

Minuet in G

Repeated notes

DANIEL TÜRK
No. 6 from "Anfängerstücke für Klavier"

Relay Race

Legato and staccato in both hands

BÉLA BARTÓK
No. 5 from "First Term at the Piano"

6

On the Playground

*Broken chord accompaniment and
two and three note figures*

BÉLA BARTÓK
No. 7 from "First Term at the Piano"

Carousel

Parallel motion between the hands

KONRAD KUNZ
Op. 14, No. 19

*Play the 1st ending and take the repeat, then play the 2nd ending, skipping over the first ending.

Evening Song

Imitation, phrase groups

KONRAD KUNZ
Op. 14, No. 106

Running in a Circle

Imitation, two-note phrases

KONRAD KUNZ
Op. 14, No. 92

Wilderness Adventure
Polyphonic playing

BÉLA BARTÓK
No. 6 from "First Term at the Piano"

Roller Blading

Singing tone in the right hand,
softer left hand accompaniment

CARL CZERNY
No. 13 from "Erster Anfang"

Moderato

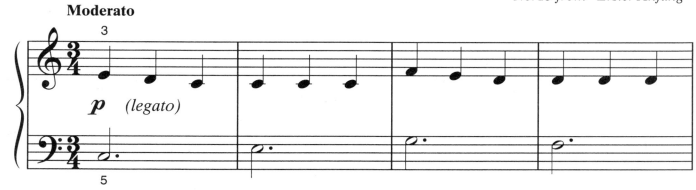

Taxi Ride

Legato, parallel and contrary motion

BÉLA BARTÓK
No. 2 from "First Term at the Piano"

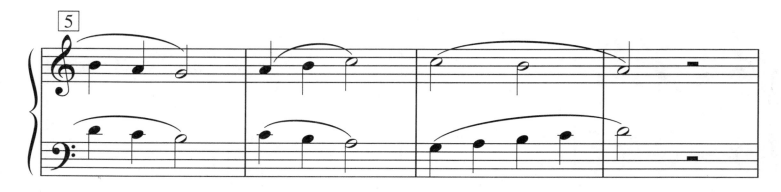

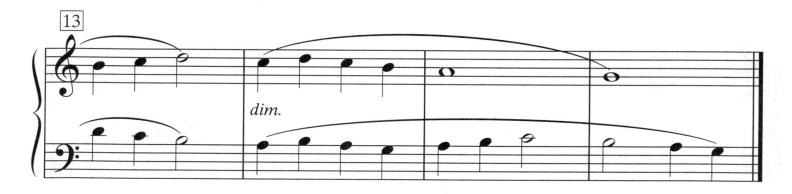

Bike Riding

Legato passages

FERDINAND BEYER
Op. 101, No. 39

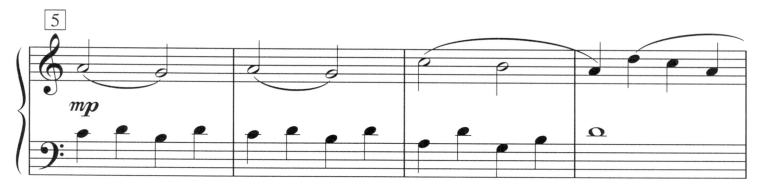

12

The Music Box

Broken chord accompaniment,
bringing out the melodic line, balance

CARL CZERNY
No. 14 from "Erster Anfang"

*For a music box sound, play both hands one octave higher.

ELM00035A

rit.

Ice Skating

Long legato phrases

FERDINAND BEYER
Op. 101, No. 35

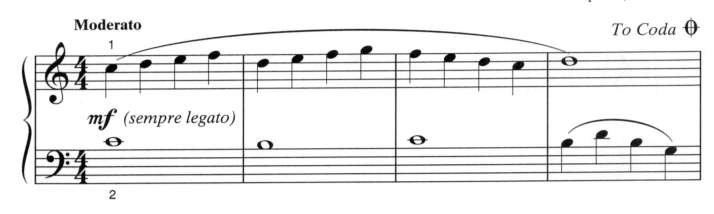

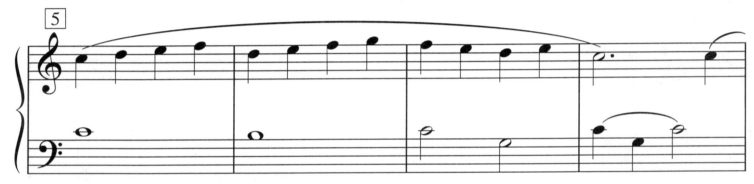

*D.C. al Coda (Da Capo al Coda) means "from the top to the *Coda*." Return to the beginning and play to
To Coda ⊕ , then jump to the ⊕ *Coda* (ending).

Melody

Staccato and legato, C five-finger pattern,
broken chord accompaniment

CARL CZERNY
Op. 777, No. 3

Joyous Reunion

Right hand staccato,
long legato phrasing in left hand

CORNELIUS GURLITT
Op. 210, No. 3

*The editor changed the original $\frac{2}{4}$ time signature to $\frac{4}{4}$ thereby eliminating sixteenth notes.

Two-By-Two

Three-note phrases, legato thirds

FERDINAND BEYER
Op. 101, No. 68

Dialogue

Five-finger legato, canonic imitiation,
terraced dynamics

BÉLA BARTÓK
No. 3. from "First Term at the Piano"

Copy Cat

Imitation, melodic shaping

CORNELIUS GURLITT
Op. 82, No. 17

*Dynamic markings are editorial.

ELM00035A

On the Swing

Left hand circular wrist motion,
right hand two-note phrases with drop-roll motion

HERMANN BERENS
Op. 70, No. 9

*The original meter of $\frac{3}{8}$ was changed to $\frac{3}{4}$ by the editor. Dynamics are editorial.

Marching

Blocked and broken chords, repeated notes,
balance between the hands

CARL CZERNY
Op. 823, No. 11

*Dynamics are editorial.
**Smaller hands may eliminate the G in the left hand.

ELM00035A

Round and Round

Major and minor hand position changes, imitation

FERDINAND BEYER
Op. 101, No. 60

*At a leisurely, moderate speed.
**Dynamic markings are editorial.

Sonatina on Five Notes

Unison playing, repeated notes, dynamic contrasts

OSKAR BOLCK

Dancing

Contrast between legato and non legato,
phrase groups of different lengths

CORNELIUS GURLITT
Op. 210, No. 6